The Charter School Teacher's Guide

to Understanding Homeschool and Parent-led Learning

Nina Elena

ZAMIZ PRESS

Education & Reference > Education > Charter Schools

Education & Reference > Education > Home Schooling

Special discounts are available on quantity purchases by corporations, associations and others. For details contact the author.

DO YOU HAVE A MESSAGE TO SHARE WITH THE WORLD? ARE YOU INTERESTED IN HAVING YOUR BOOK PUBLISHED? VISIT ZAMIZPRESS.COM

No part of this publication may be reproduced, distributed or transmitted in any form or by any means, including photocopying, recording, or other electronic or mechanical methods, without the prior written permission of the publisher, except in the case of brief quotations embodied in critical reviews and certain other noncommercial uses permitted by copyright law.

Copyright © 2023 Nina Elena. All rights reserved.

Editing: Rebecca Black

The Charter School Teacher's Guide to Understanding Homeschool and Parent-led Learning/ Nina Elena

ISBN: 978-1-949813-40-1

Contents

1. WHAT IS HOMESCHOOLING? — 1
   Are Homeschool Students up to Par? — 2
   What is Real Homeschooling? — 3
   Is Homeschooling Worth it? — 4
   Are all Homeschoolers the Same? — 9

2. GETTING TO KNOW HOMESCHOOLING — 17
   Is Non-Charter Homeschooling Legal? — 17
   Why is Homeschooling Good? — 18
   Should Parents Have a Schedule or be More Relaxed? — 20
   What Does a Homeschool Day Look Like? — 21

3. WHAT ARE THE DIFFERENT WAYS TO HOMESCHOOL? — 31
   Traditional Method — 32
   Charlotte Mason Method — 33
   Unschooling — 34
   Classical Education — 35
   Pods — 37
   What is a Co-op? — 38

4. CHOOSING CURRICULUM & IDENTIFYING LEARNING STYLES — 41
   How Should Parents Pick Curriculum? Ask Them: — 41
   Are Homeschool Kids in the Same Grade Level as Public School? — 49
   Should Parents Buy New or Used Books? — 50

Tips to Give Parents to Make Homeschooling Easier	55
Are There any Curriculums You Recommend?	58
Extra Information	64

5. SHOULD THE HOUSE LOOK LIKE A SCHOOL? ... 67

How do Parents Create a Learning Environment?	67
Are There Community Resources for Homeschoolers?	71
What is a Homeschool Convention?	72

6. HOW CAN PARENTS MAKE SURE HOMESCHOOL IS SUCCESSFUL? ... 75

Are You Saying You Run Your Home Like a Business?	75
How Can Parents Know if They're Doing it Right?	78
What Can Parents do While Waiting for Materials to Arrive?	79
What is Deschooling?	80

7. ARE HOMESCHOOLED KIDS SOCIALIZED? ... 83

Are Homeschoolers Uncool?	83
If They Build it, Will They Come?	85

8. HELPING PARENTS HANDLE HARD DAYS ... 87

How Can I Guide Parent who Homeschool Multiple Kids at the Same Time?	90
What About Parents With Children with Special Needs?	91
How Can I Help Parents Who Feel Overwhelmed?	92
What if Their Child Can't Focus?	95

What About Parents with an Only Child?	96
What Should Parents Teach at Each Stage?	97

9. IS IT POSSIBLE TO HOMESCHOOL WELL IN HIGH SCHOOL? — 99

What Challenges Does High School Present? — 99

10. WHAT ELSE DO I NEED TO KNOW? — 105

Afterword: Can You Just Tell Parents What to do?	109
About the Author	111
Recommended Reading	113
Endnotes	117

Chapter 1

What is Homeschooling?

By the end of this book, you will know all about homeschooling and parent-led learning. You'll know the legalities, the lingo and just what to do in each circumstance.

After reading this, you could put on a movie that shows homeschooling in a positive light. Three great movies are *RV*, starring Robin Williams, *Mom's Night Out*, starring Sean Astin, and *Courageous*, starring Alex Kendrick.

I will introduce you to people, books and resources that will give you the tools you need for success, one of these people is Vicki Bentley.

Vicki is a rockstar in the homeschool community. She makes it look effortless, which is a testimony to how much effort she put in. While I have homeschooled for 17 years, Vicki has homeschooled 17 children. She brings a special wisdom and perspective. She is the mother of eight daughters and has also been a foster mom to over fifty children. Now she is a grandmother to 23 grandchildren and 10 great-grandchildren. She has addressed state and national homeschool conventions, as well as speaking to university teacher organizations.

Look for Vicki's homeschool insights in her "Vicki Says" segments that begin with her picture and end with this ∼ symbol.

Throughout this book I will share factual information, as well as insights and ideas. The ideas I share and the personal examples I give are not meant to tell anyone exactly what to do. My hope is that they will get you thinking about ways to create your own versions that are unique to the families you work with. I can tell you what's worked for us, but my goal is to inspire you to look at homeschooling in a new way.

Are Homeschool Students up to Par?

Is one of your concerns that your students won't be at the same educational level as their public-school friends?

When moments of doubt creep into your mind, remember these statistics. In 2022, 93% of Baltimore students in third through eighth grade tested below grade level in math. 23 of those Baltimore schools didn't have a single child test at grade level[1]. Not one.

Across the country a 13-year-old Ukrainian refugee asked to return to war ravaged Ukraine, rather than stay in the dangerous San Francisco school she attended[2].

The San Francisco Examiner reported in January that another school had, "students recording videos of themselves as they beat another student, three female students assaulting a special-education student, and a student bringing an air gun to school—all without documented suspensions at the time of those incidents."[3]

Charter and homeschooling parents have made a great choice.

What is Real Homeschooling?

When I talk about homeschooling, I mean giving children a comprehensive education at home. This might also be called traditional homeschooling. It includes teaching the four core subjects of **math, history, language arts,** and **science.** In high school we would also include electives.

I am not referring to virtual learning, take home packets, home instruction due to chronic illness or pandemic learning. Those are not homeschooling.

We will talk about other methods of homeschooling in chapter 3. For now, I just want you to understand how I use the word homeschool.

One of the most common questions charter school teachers ask is, "Are parents qualified to homeschool their children?" There are successful homeschool parents who are high school dropouts or who barely speak the language. Some homeschooling moms have chronic illnesses and teach school from bed while friends bring their child on field trips. There are also homeschool parents who are molecular biologists, doctors, EMTs and lawyers. Where there's a will, there's a way. Any parent who loves their children enough to research how to homeschool them and then does what is necessary to educate their children, is qualified.

You can encourage brand new charter homeschool parents to look online for meetups, support groups, classes and park play days for their kids. They need to find and start going to these before they're in desperate need of social time and even before they feel ready. The day is coming when both the parents and children will desperately need the support of people who are doing parent-led learning. They will need the encouragement from other moms, and their children will need the camaraderie and laughter of other kids.

When I began homeschooling our children, I sought advice and mentorship from people who had been homeschooling for long enough to graduate some of their children. I wanted to see the finished product. Had anyone been doing this long enough to have adult children who were successful and well-rounded?

Is Homeschooling Worth it?

There are many stories of homeschool families with children who graduated college with a bachelor's degree in physics at age 13, such as Elliott Tanner. He is now pursuing his PhD. Elliot enrolled in college at age 9.

Another family, Kip and Mona Lisa Harding, have ten children and each has graduated high school by the age of 12.

In fact, many Ivy league universities are actively recruiting homeschooled students due to their knowledge, intelligence, and ability to work independently.

"'The high achievement level of homeschoolers is readily recognized by recruiters from some of the best colleges in the nation,' said Dr. Susan Berry, who researches and writes about educational topics like the fast-growing rate of homeschooling. 'Schools such as Massachusetts Institute of Technology, Harvard, Stanford, and Duke University all actively recruit homeschoolers.'"[4]

Some homeschool graduates forgo college and turn their high school side business into full-time entrepreneurship. Others take their high school apprenticeships and become full-time skilled labor, making forty dollars an hour.

My goal for our children was to have them graduate high school with all the skills they would need to support themselves in the adult world. What they decided to do with their adult lives would be their decision. Besides a great education, I wanted them to have good financial knowledge, the ability to write well, great interpersonal skills, a willingness to learn, and one entire skill-set they could monetize. I choose the skill set based on their strengths. Our oldest excelled in writing and loved to organize. She would make the perfect executive assistant. That meant her electives were in Microsoft Word, Office,

Excel, and PowerPoint. When she graduated, she was fully qualified to walk into any office and get a position.

Our son had different strengths, so by the time he graduated high school, his strengths in robotics, electronics, communication, and arithmetic, prepared him to walk into any technical industry and talk his way into a position.

Both of our older children attended community college on-campus while in high school. This allowed them the opportunity to see the college atmosphere in small snippets and to graduate from high school with college credits.

I loved hearing the stories they told of college professors asking them, "How do you know so much? Were you homeschooled?"

Some affirmed them with, "You're the only one who is paying attention in class." Or, "You're my best student!"

It was validating to hear that our commitment to education and personal responsibility made them stand out in a college classroom of high school graduates and older adult students.

An early introduction to college gave our kids confidence in their abilities. They both had lots of friends throughout their homeschool years and made many more at college. I am constantly amazed at their mental strength and character. Are they perfect? No. But neither are we. We are incredibly proud of the people they have become and have never looked back on a single day of homeschooling and regretted our decision.

How parents craft their homeschool is a personal decision. As Jordan Peterson says, "You're going to pay a price for every bloody thing you do and everything you don't do. You don't get to choose to not pay a price. You get to choose which poison you're going to take. That's it."[5]

Even with good intentions, homeschooling parents and charter school teachers are each going to make mistakes and those mistakes will cost us. But when we look back at our decisions, we can judge them based on two criteria:

1. Did we make the best decision we could with the information we had at the time?

2. Did we do what was best and stick with it when it got hard? Or did we give up and do what was easy?

As Zig Ziglar says, "I'll do today what other people won't, so I can have tomorrow what other people can't."[6]

Parenting is hard and homeschool parenting is even harder, but the rewards are endless.

Each person walks into homeschooling with their own set of issues to overcome. Homeschool family life will change, free time will change and where parents put their focus will change. Parents will need to brush up on child psychology, stages of development, and learning styles.

There are also preconceived notions we each carry around. Moms may have to drop the wall they've put up to protect themselves from catty moms at the pickup line with fancy coffees and designer handbags.

Homeschool moms come in all shapes and sizes. Some hike with their kids, some buy things at Walmart, and many don't always wear makeup. Some make a lot of money and hire private tutors. Others have no money and make their curriculum from scratch just like they make their bread.

Homeschooling is the great equalizer. It's a very diverse bunch of families who have one goal in mind, the best for their children. If moms spend enough time with other homeschool parents they will find someone in the group they click with. They will also find someone who is a great mentor. It just takes time.

A good place to start is with a set of goals. Let's put our heads together to create a list of goals the parents you work with can create for their children. Have them write down:

1. Your life goals for your children

(Example: I want my children to know enough to succeed in any situation, know how to learn what they don't know, be kind to others, be strong leaders and share their convictions with others.)

2. Your educational goals for your children

(Example: My children will have an extensive knowledge of _____ [maybe language or science or history]. They will have a firm grasp of _____ [maybe math or reading or Spanish]. And they will know enough _____ (language/science/ math/ history) not to feel stupid.

3. A family motto

(Example: "To go where no man has gone before" -Star Trek)

4. In a perfect world, what would you want for your children?

Are all Homeschoolers the Same?

Our priorities have always been for our children to 1. become strong readers; 2. be excellent communicators; 3. have a working knowledge of math and science; 4. have a love of history; and 5. use logic and critical thinking to analyze information. Why? Because we knew that if they could read with ease, they could learn anything. Understanding the world around them is important. Without math skills, they could be easily overcharged and unable to manage their own finances or business. They should also be able to communicate effectively with others in business and life. If they knew history well, they would be able to notice when history tries to repeat itself. And if they could think logically and critically about information, they would be able to see through lies.

If we were a family of engineers, perhaps our focus would be different. If we were artists or biologists, they might also be different.

There's no need to be like everyone else. Homeschoolers are an eclectic bunch.

Homeschool groups are usually very diverse. One mom wears flowing dresses and flowers in her hair while another wears yoga pants and a weave. Some families eat takeout every day and some grind their own organic wheat. It's not unusual to see a mom with blue hair laughing together with a mom in a hijab. If you can think it, there's a homeschool family to represent it and all the kids are playing together. It's a beautiful sight.

When our children graduated high school and headed to college, they needed to know how to read well and use the library for research. That way, if they make bad career choices or if the job market takes a turn for the worse, they can learn anything by reading about it. I thought that if they were excellent readers, they would have the ability to study for a new career. If the world experiences a zombie apocalypse and all electronics are gone, they can break into an abandoned library and learn any skill they need. We gave them the tools to accomplish anything. If we didn't give them the tools, they would struggle just to survive everyday life. Why would we want that for them?

As much as I love homeschooling, it surprises most moms to hear that I didn't homeschool willingly. One day my husband came to me and said that since we were going to move, I should investigate homeschooling. I was not thrilled with the idea, to put it mildly. But he was right, we were about to move and that would have meant our oldest would have spent one month in her current school. Then she would have been in a new school for a month as we lived with family while house hunting. Finally, she would have been in a third school once we bought a house. That sounded very stressful for a first grader.

My first thought was that homeschool families were weird and that I wasn't about to wear jean dresses and head coverings, so I wouldn't fit in. I'm not sure where I got that idea from, but that was my thinking.

Our pastor's family and the assistant pastor's family both homeschooled their kids. They were normal, happy families and their adult children were fantastic. I called one woman and arranged a time to go to her house. I walked in and said, "Okay, show me what this homeschooling thing is all about."

She pulled out her youngest child's schoolbooks and I was in awe. I had never seen such great school materials. I'd spent time in our oldest child's kindergarten classroom and had observed the level of instruction and materials. These homeschool materials were a thousand times better. The quality of the books, the information and the graphics made the sloppily copied papers that came home each week look like garbage. I was hooked. My child could get this level of education, a private school education, and I could do it from home at a fraction of the cost!

I immediately ordered the Abeka catalog and couldn't wait to go through it. I will explain the first mistake I made with this in chapter 10.

There was one other reservation I had about homeschooling. We have very high expectations for our children. We see how smart they are and want them to live up to their potential. Could I have the patience to teach them without being overbearing and crushing their spirits? God gave me my answer a few weeks later.

It was time for our oldest child's school assembly, and I sat on the bleachers as the classes came in. One teacher stood out as she berated the children in her class for having a foot over the line or wiggling while waiting. She was particularly harsh with her class of third graders. In that moment, I knew that even if I was too strict or expected too much from my kids, at least it would come from a place of love. My error would be that I loved them too much to let them be less than they could be. That was a potential problem I could live with.

Our daughter's first grade curriculum was ordered along with some preschool workbooks for our son, and we began our journey into homeschooling!

Three months into our journey, we settled into our new home. My husband asked when I was going to enroll our oldest in school. It was too late. We absolutely loved homeschooling and our local homeschool group, so we decided to stick with it. By the end of that first year, we all loved the homeschool life and never looked back.

Vicki Says:

Homeschooling is more than simply "school at home." It's not even really an education choice–it's a lifestyle choice. Homeschooling is just one aspect of *home discipleship*. The Greek model of education was founded on pursuit of knowledge, but the Hebrew model of education was founded on pursuit of relationship.[1] I encourage you to connect with your child, to convey to him that your love for him is not dependent upon how fast he can finish his math work or how many science experiments he does a week.

Another second-generation homeschool mom has gradually grown to appreciate–after becoming a mom herself–the good intentions of her own imperfect parents and the benefits of homeschooling, even though she balked at cooperating in middle school and even the teen years.

"The thinking behind my refusing to do school during that time? I'm pretty sure it was mostly stubborn rebellion. Taking a stand against my mom personally and trying to give her as hard a time as possible as our relationship deteriorated."

But she also introspectively notes, when asked what her mom could have done differently:

"I think somehow, she missed the mark on finding a way to truly connect with me and act towards me in a way that made me feel seen and heard and understood while I was younger... and then that chance passed for us as I started turning into a teenager and developing rebellious habits and attitude so that she had to address all of that junk instead of focusing on building a better connection.

So, I think the key to a successful homeschool relationship with your child is to absolutely make sure that you are building that *emotional and personal connection* way before and throughout the actual schoolwork process. I just feel like we never hit that connection properly and the rest fell apart from there..."

Thankfully, she and her mom are now working on restoring the lost years.

Life is messy. Homeschooling isn't the answer to all your family's problems.[2] Folks, it doesn't matter if your kids can solve quadratic equations–if they can hardly wait to get out of your house, and then don't ever want to talk to you again. Build connections. I wasn't a very joyful mom for quite a few years, but eventually realized I had allowed God's enemy to rob me of my joy. So, I had to be purposeful about building connections with my kids, about "tying lovestrings" from my heart to theirs.[3] I encourage you to be intentional.

WHEN PARENTS HAVE time to sit down and figure out which brands of curriculum to buy for each subject, they need to pick things that excite them and think will work well for their kids. Teaching is often a transference of feeling from one person to another. In homeschooling that means that if the parents is fascinated by history or math, their enthusiasm will rub off and the kids will enjoy it as well because the parent made it come alive. But if the parent absolutely hates a subject, that can come across as well. That's not a feeling you want to transfer. So that would be a great subject to farm out to an online course or a local in-person class.

If the parent feels that way about every subject, then it's probably time to sit down and think about some more serious things, like the questions at the beginning of this chapter. They are going to have to roll up their sleeves and do some deep work to prepare themselves and their family.

There is also learning curve to staying home with children.

Chapter 2

Getting to Know Homeschooling

Is Non-Charter Homeschooling Legal?

"Homeschooling has been legal throughout the United States for about 25 years, but regulations vary dramatically by state. Only two states require background checks for parents who choose to homeschool, and just ten require parents to have a high school degree. Fewer than half require any kind of evaluation or testing of homeschooled children."[7]

"While some states have a special homeschooling option for parents who are certified teachers, no state requires that every homeschooling parent be a certified teacher.

In fact, research has found little difference between the academic achievement of homeschooled students whose parents were certified teachers and those whose parents were not. They both scored on average much higher than their counterparts in public school."⁸

One of the main reasons that homeschooling is an option for families is due to the tireless work of the Homeschool Legal Defense Association (HSLDA). For 40 years they have fought to keep homeschooling legal and defend parents and children from government overreach. We have been members for about 15 years and I recommend that you look into membership. You can visit them at HSLDA.org to find out more.

Why is Homeschooling Good?

Not only can't our kids read, write, or count very well; now they can't drive a nail, plane a board, use a saw, turn a screwdriver, boil an egg, or find ways to amuse themselves and stay healthy. -John Taylor Gatto

In his excellent book *Weapons of Mass Instruction*, John Taylor Gatto states;

"The same young people we confine to classrooms these days once cleared this continent when it was a wilderness, built roads, canals, cities; whipped the greatest military power of earth not once but twice, sold ice to faraway India before refrigeration, and produced so many miracles—from the six-shooter to the steamboat to manned flight—that America spread glimmerings of what open-sourced creativity could do all around the planet...

"Don't let your [children] have their childhoods

extended, not even for a day. If David Farragut could take command of a captured British warship as a preteen, if Ben Franklin could apprentice himself to a printer at the same age...there's no telling what your own kids could do. After a long life, and thirty years in the public school trenches, I've concluded that genius is as common as dirt. We suppress genius because we haven't yet figured out how to manage a population of educated men and women. The solution, I think, is simple and glorious. Let them manage themselves."[9]

In a 2016 survey by the Department of Education "the highest percentage of homeschooled students had parents who said that a concern about the environment of other schools, such as safety, drugs, or negative peer pressure was one reason to homeschool (80 percent). The highest percentage of students' parents reported that among all reasons, a concern about the environment of other schools was the most important reason for homeschooling (34 percent). Seventeen percent of homeschooled students had parents who reported dissatisfaction with academic instruction at other schools as the most important reason for homeschooling, while 16 percent reported a desire to provide religious instruction as the most important reason for homeschooling (table 8)."[10]

When new homeschooling families ask about choosing curriculum for their children, the first thing experienced homeschool moms ask is, "How does your child learn?" or "What does your child like to do?" (Video games and playing with friends are not the correct answers.)

Most new charter school parents will not know these answers.

We are asking about that child's strengths and weaknesses. To know those, parents will need to spend a lot of time with their child in different learning environments. If they were previously out of the house eight hours a day, five days a week, that type of observation probably didn't happen.

Parents saw them in the morning rushing to school. They saw them exhausted at the end of the day. They saw them on the weekends and on school breaks, but may not have spent the kind of learning time and down time that would allow anyone to answer those questions. Now they will have the time to discover the answers to those questions.

Homeschool students doing traditional homeschooling consistently test one grade or more above their public-school peers. This doesn't mean that will be the result from the first year of charter homeschooling, but those who homeschool over time will.

Should Parents Have a Schedule or be More Relaxed?

I recommend starting with a schedule. It is so much easier to begin with a schedule and then back off, than to start off easy and try to get your kids to cooperate.

I recommend starting each school day at the same time. This will stop a lot of whining and complaining once it becomes a habit. Some families start school at 8am, some at 9am and some at 10am. It all depends on the family.

What Does a Homeschool Day Look Like?

Laura's Day:

We don't follow a specific schedule in our homeschool, but posted on the refrigerator is a reminder of our goal:

To Have Our Best Day

- Everyone brings their best attitude
- Be dressed and ready by 9 am
- Start the day with breakfast and prayer
- Chores and school before play
- Eat healthy meals at proper times
- Practice piano and violin
- Prep clothes and supplies for the next day
- All dishes done before bed

I've found that the closer we can stick to these simple goals, the more likely we are to have a calm and productive day.

After morning chores my slow-moving-in-the-morning 11th grader usually spends some time practicing piano before heading to her room to work on her lessons. I check in with her from time to time to make sure she's staying on task and not getting too distracted by her phone or whatever art project she's currently working on. She works independently and has due dates for each chapter or unit in her various subjects. When the due date arrives, she has to turn in her work and take the test, ready or not. We used to be more lenient with deadlines but have come to realize the hard deadline is important motivation for completing her work in a timely manner; this stricter system is working better for both of us.

I always remind my 7th grader to do math first while her brain is freshest. Throughout the day, she checks in with me after each subject or anytime she has questions. We do history read alouds and science projects together, but otherwise she works pretty independently. She has a list of subjects to work through each day (not every subject every day), but she doesn't sit still at a desk to work through the list, that's just not how she functions. She can often be found reading her history book in a blanket fort with the guinea pig on her chest or writing an essay on the tree swing while her little sister digs holes nearby.

Play is learning for my preschooler. And no, I don't mean every toy or game is "educational" or every activity is planned with an agenda. Her play is almost completely unstructured. I do set out a few stations at the kitchen table sometimes: a seasonal sensory bin, play dough, letter recognition or counting activities from her school box, peg boards with rubber bands, etc. But that is all completely voluntary. Some days she'll spend a long time working through everything I put out. Other times she'll just do one, request something else, or ignore them altogether. Structured school will come gradually as she becomes developmentally ready for it. Right now, we read lots of books together, run errands and do chores, and play, play, play.

It's important to me that the big girls try to have their lessons wrapped up by the time Dad gets home at 4. The dynamic of our home changes at that point with dinner preparations, everyone wanting to talk to Dad, getting ready for the kids' various evening activities and looking ahead to the next day. If they need additional time for any schoolwork, we usually try to fit that in on Saturday, but even for my high schooler that's the exception, not the norm.

I've also learned we function best if we limit scheduled activities outside the house (during school hours) to one or two days a week. Any more than that and too much of our time at home is taken up with housework, so it's hard to get into a productive rhythm with school. By being careful to limit participation in weekly co-ops, lessons, and park days to something we can manage without pushing our limits, I'm able to leave some flexibility to add in the occasional field trip or errands.

Jessica's Day:

We don't follow a strict schedule, but having a consistent routine or flow is necessary. I notice my kids are more cooperative when they know what to expect from the day. With that in mind, I outline this timeline based on what usually happens, not what I have imposed as the schedule.

This routine has changed over the years based on the number of kids we have, ages, times of extra activities, my own health, my husband's work schedule, etc. We know when it's working and when it's not. When it's not, we change things up. Having this flexibility is one of the most beautiful things about homeschooling!

At 8am I wake the older two kids, the only ones who prefer to sleep in. All the little ones are usually awake by then and eager to start breakfast. This is a firm time, but it is the only thing in the morning that always happens exactly at that time.

Everyone helps prepare breakfast, or watches toddlers or babies while we work. By 8:30, we are usually all sitting down. I might read aloud, or we may listen to a podcast or audiobook during breakfast, but not always.

By around 9:30, breakfast is over. I send everyone to do self-care, and one home care task. Self-care includes brushing teeth, getting dressed if they aren't already, brushing hair, etc. Home care means unloading clean dishes (dirty dishes get done later), clearing and wiping the table, and other tasks that help us move toward starting school for the day—not highly involved tasks.

10am is "table time". Table time work is skill level work like math, handwriting, spelling, and phonics. During table time, I have the older kids take turns rotating on toddler care. I set out an activity, toy, or books for them to engage the 1- and 3-year-old with. It's amazing how well even my

6-year-old can entertain them! I usually give the youngest school-aged child my attention first, since their work gets done the most quickly, then work up to the oldest.

Most of the time our table work is done by lunchtime. The kids take turns making or helping with lunch. Usually, we watch an educational program or go outside for lunch. This is MY break time! I read, eat, or do my housework during this time.

If we don't have any activities for the day, our content work like history, science and social studies gets done in the late afternoon or evening when Dad is home. This is usually in the form of reading, followed by narration or discussion. This happens typically three times per week. Other afternoons we are socializing with friends at the park, at the library, at chess club, or at a sports meet up.

Our morning routine, including table time, is Monday-Friday. Although only the oldest two get table time done on Thursday when the other kids are getting ready for and attending a daytime gymnastics class. Their school for the day is usually only audiobooks or educational songs in the car. Four days a week still provides the consistency we need to make steady progress on their math and reading skills.

I want to add all of our curriculum is "open and go" meaning I don't have to do much prep before the school day starts. I also don't plan a certain amount of pages or problems each day, but instead track what's done. Some days or weeks a child may move slowly through math but speed through phonics. As long as effort is being made each day, I'm content. In this way a lot of pressure is taken off of them and me, and I'm certain over time they make just as much progress and retain more because I don't push their pace. Another perk of that homeschool flexibility!

MY DAY:

I have a lot to do each day and I also value alone time. My days are structured to give me both time to accomplish everything and time to myself. I get up at 5am and spend the first two hours having a cup of tea, working at my business, exercising, and taking a shower. Our youngest gets up around 7, so that's when the day begins.

At 9am school starts.

We start the day with the most difficult subjects. Our brains are the most alert and able to handle the strain first thing in the school day. We've tried mixing it up, but this has been the best solution for us.

Then it's lunch time.

After lunch time it is recess outside or play time in their room for 1 hour. This gives us some wiggle time before more schoolwork, and it gives me a mental break.

Whenever time is mentioned, set a timer. If you don't, then your kids will come and ask you if the time is up every five minutes, making it a miserable time for both of you. Alternately, one of you will lose track of time. Losing track of time means school doesn't get done until 8 pm and you're both fried. You can avoid these problems by either turning on your phone's timer or getting a cheap kitchen timer that ticks as it moves and makes a loud ding. (A ticking kitchen timer is especially helpful when you first try this as it helps younger kids who need a visual representation of time.)

After the lunch break, it's time for whichever subjects didn't get done before lunch. I'm usually folding laundry, cooking, or cleaning the house. My job is to listen, correct any wrong words, ask and answer questions.

It might look like this:

Billy: In 1692 Colob sailed the ocean

Mom: Columbus

Billy: Columbus sailed the ocean from Spain to...

ANOTHER EXAMPLE IS:

Billy: Ben Franklin said, "Those who would give up essential liberty, to purchase a little temporary safety, deserve neither liberty nor safety."

Mom: That was great reading, now stop for a second. Why do you think Mr. Franklin said that?

If I notice my child is having trouble concentrating during a particular subject, I may ask them to unload the dishwasher or sweep outside for a few minutes to give them an excuse to get up and move, before returning to the subject at hand.

Here is our sample school day:

9:00 math

9:40 history

10:15 language

11:00 lunch

11:45 break time

12:45 art
1:45 science
2:00 school is finished

Vicki Says:

Children are generally *born curious*; they are created to learn. They tend to naturally explore and investigate and learn. But learning and schooling aren't necessarily the same thing.

In the earlier years, even up into primary school, *I won't* usually means *I can't* or *I'm not ready for this yet*. But he doesn't generally know how to process or communicate that, so it sometimes comes out as *I don't want to!* Or even *I'm going to slide from my chair to the floor in a sobbing mess*. (Or maybe that's his mom.)

So, what *is* age- or developmentally appropriate for a younger child? Some children read at age four, while others jump into phonics around age eight—and both can be in the range of normal! Children mature at different rates and focus on different skills at different seasons, and there are a lot of factors to take into consideration.[4] Most children sort of "level out" around third grade, but before that, hold all those scope-and-sequence checklists very loosely, and think of learning as a continuum, not an age-specific menu. They don't need scholastic deadlines. They *do* need lots of outdoor or free play and real-life learning.

Outdoor or Free Play

Pediatric occupational therapist Angela Hanscom "discovered that movement through active play, particularly in the outdoors, is absolutely the most beneficial gift we as parents, teachers and caregivers can bestow on our children to ensure healthy bodies, creative minds, academic success, emotional stability, and strong social skills. Children should be getting daily movement experiences throughout the day in order to develop strong and healthy musculoskeletal systems. Musculoskeletal and sensory systems lay the groundwork for higher level mental and physical skills as children age. Ideally, kids of all ages should get at least three hours of free play outdoors a day."[5]

Real-life Learning

If nobody told you that they had to go to school at age 5, what would you be doing with them?[6] What are you doing with them now? Try doing that same thing, but a bit more intentionally. Interact with them naturally—you don't have to invent lots of artificial learning experiences—you have plenty of "real" ones already! (Don't believe me? Check out the articles in the notes at the end of this book, and be sure to read Durenda Wilson's book, *The Unhurried*

Homeschooler; it's a quick read–I read it in the hour my banana bread baked!)

So, when your younger student is balking at that new concept you are trying to introduce, first ask yourself if he is *ready* for this new concept; if not, maybe let it go for now and circle back in a few days or weeks. Second, is there a play-based or relevant-in-real-life way to introduce it to him? Or maybe try the strewing method[7] that one mama uses with her four boys: leaving books or activities lying around the house for the kids to find so they think it's *their* idea to try them out!

Chapter 3

What are the Different Ways to Homeschool?

"**Pedagogy** refers to the methods, practices, and purposes of teaching; **curriculum** is what is specifically being taught."
-Pete Hegseth, *Battle for the American Mind*

Pete also wrote that the word **paidagogos** generally means "a leader who walks with students and trains them in manners, academics, and virtue."[11] That's what parents are trying to do. Parents are walking with their children through their formative years and training them to have knowledge, character, and manners.

Character training is teaching children to have "moral excellence and firmness."[12] We teach them what is right and what is wrong in life. For example, it's right to help your neighbor and it's wrong to steal. This must be taught to children and shown by example in everyday life.

As families evaluate each type of homeschool method they should look for ones that will nurture positive personality traits in each of their children.

Traditional Method

There are several ways that families homeschool. There is the traditional method which I talked about in the beginning, which is educating children at home with things such as textbooks, workbooks, readers, and a program. This program can be designed either by the parent or by a curriculum provider and would cover math, history, science, language arts and any electives.

Pros: Ensures parents teach all subjects, gives a quality education, rewards children who enjoy seeing how well they are doing, has workbooks for ease of use, identifies a grade level, is great for showing grandparents how well your children are doing in school.

Cons: May be less hands-on, requires reading and writing, is more structured, looks more like regular school.

Charlotte Mason Method

Then there is the Charlotte Mason method. SimplyCharlotteMason.com describes this as, "Charlotte Mason education is three-pronged: in her words, 'Education is an Atmosphere, a Discipline, a Life.'

Charlotte believed that the ideas that rule your life as the parent make up one-third of a children's education.

By 'Discipline,' Charlotte meant the discipline of good habits—and specifically habits of character.

The other third of education, 'Life,' applies to academics. Charlotte believed that we should give children living thoughts and ideas, not just dry facts."[13]

This is a great approach for some people and can be the perfect fit for both the mom teaching it and the children learning it.

Pros: More relaxed, includes a lot of hands-on and outside activities, uses regular books instead of textbooks or workbooks, doesn't require finding a specific grade level.

Cons: Too relaxed for some families, can lack structure, may not appeal to children who enjoy getting rewards for work well done, may not appeal to parents who want to show work to family members.

Unschooling

The unschooling method is also called "child-led learning". Unschooling doesn't have an actual definition, so I can only tell you from 17 years of homeschool experience what unschooling has looked like to me. Unschooling has its time and place and there are variations of unschooling and traditional schooling that merge, so this is just a general overview so you understand this option and can answer about it intelligently.

Just like there are different types of homeschoolers, there are also different types of unschoolers. Some do a more child-led type of instruction where they allow their children to choose what they are interested in. It can look like anything from allowing your science-minded son to wake up and head outside to study the ecosystem of a stream; or in contrast a parent who only teaches what the child asks to learn.

An unschooling educational environment can work for the family of a child with an especially high IQ. This child is the one who you might find on the living room floor surrounded by books on how to code a robot. If your child wakes up and starts whining about playing video games, this is NOT a viable option.

Some unschooling families call themselves unschoolers, but their houses are full of educational materials, and they still have formal math and language instruction. This might look like each child in a different math textbook, but for the rest of the subjects, they encourage the kids to get books from the library, research on their own and go on field trips to learn.

Pros: Unschooling allows advanced children to race ahead without the burden of set subjects or particular levels. It is also advantageous for the free-spirited nature lover who never comes inside.

Cons: Parents who don't value education may use the term unschooling to excuse a lack of education for their children or for lazy parenting. This has not been the case with any of the unschooling families I have encountered. However, this is not a good fit for parents who need accountability to make education happen. If the child loves workbook pages and rewards this probably isn't a good choice for them. Children who love to get an A on a test and feel proud of their academic accomplishments, should have that opportunity.

Classical Education

Susan Wise Bauer describes the classical education model as, "a three-part process of training the mind. The early years of school are spent in absorbing facts, systematically laying the foundations for advanced study. In the middle grades, students learn to think through arguments. In the high school years, they learn to express themselves. This classical pattern is called the trivium."[14]

There are classical education programs for homeschoolers that meet weekly, such as Classical Conversations. You can also purchase classical education curriculum online through Memoria Press or Classical Academic Press. Other homeschool publishers such as The Well-Trained Mind are built on the classical education model.

Classical Academic Press explains classical education as the teaching of liberal arts. On their website they ask, "What are the liberal arts? They are grammar, logic, rhetoric (the verbal arts of the trivium), arithmetic, geometry, music, and astronomy (the mathematical arts of the quadrivium). This approach to education also includes the study of Latin. The classical approach teaches students how to learn and how to think."[15]

PROS: There are many positives to pursuing a classical education. Students who have a classical education are generally articulate, knowledgeable about history, and know great works of literature. They can also think critically and understand how to use logic to analyze information.

CONS: Many families find the workload of the classical education model to be overwhelming. The topics introduced in the literature is not always considered age appropriate and introducing mythological gods and goddesses can be confusing to children. Parents for whom

English is a second language may find classical education materials too difficult to use.

Pods

Pod schooling is not new, but interest in it has increased dramatically over the past three years. Like unschooling, pods do not have a dictionary definition. When someone talks about starting a homeschool pod, they are usually referring to gathering several families together to pay a teacher to instruct their children several days a week. It is similar to the one-room schoolhouse model.

This has been a good option for families where both parents work and have several friends who want to pod school together. This might look like six seventh-grade students renting a room to have class together from 9am-3pm Monday through Thursday.

I have watched people attempt to form pods, but the individuality of homeschool families and the need to follow the same curriculum, makes this a hard model to get off the ground.

Pros: This option appeals to parents who need their children to be out of the home for most of the day and want them to be with their peers.

. . .

Cons: Pods lack the individualized curriculum that makes homeschool so appealing, it also requires the participants to be around the same age and of similar socio-economic status, to afford the same materials.

What is a Co-op?

Co-ops are cooperative teaching groups for homeschool families. Each one is established by one or two homeschool families who want to get their kids together for certain subjects. Some co-ops are run as formal organizations.

Formal co-ops usually have written agreements that families must sign. These agreements are similar to agreements you might see on a sports team. They go over the structure of the co-op, what the participation rules are, and the code of conduct. There is also a fee each student pays for renting the facility, insurance, supplies, snacks, and any payment given to the parents who teach the classes. Classes at a formal co-op might include language arts, pre-algebra, American history, art, logic, Spanish, or drama. Some formal co-ops are drop-off classes and some require a parent to stay in the building.

These formal co-ops often have credentialed teachers who teach some classes and many require parents to volunteer in a certain number of classes. Classes are normally one to two semesters long.

The type of co-op that is more frequently seen is several homeschool families who decide to get together to cooperatively have classes they enjoy teaching. This might look like six homeschool families meeting at a house or church to have an art class and science class once a week. The parents either take turns teaching or helping in the class. There is usually a small fee to cover supplies. After class there is a group lunch picnic.

These informal co-ops give kids a chance to learn from someone who is passionate about a particular subject and attending helps facilitate friendships for the kids and the parents. We have enjoyed being part of both types of co-ops.

If there is a subject I'm lazy about doing or if it's a particularly hard time such as a new baby or a move, then I enroll my children in a formal co-op class or buy a video program for that subject. That way I can ensure my children will learn that subject.

Chapter 4

Choosing Curriculum & Identifying Learning Styles

There are hundreds of homeschool curriculum packages available. Helping families find the ones that suit their children is harder than it sounds.

How Should Parents Pick Curriculum? Ask Them:

1. What are your worries as you begin homeschooling?

Do you worry that you won't do a good enough job? That your children may not get the best education? That your mother-in-law thinks your children will be uneducated? Or that your ex-husband doesn't think homeschoolers are properly socialized? These answers change what I would recommend. In those cases, I recommend a more structured homeschool curriculum such as Abeka for your first year. This is so you can get used to how homeschool works, get a lot of guidance through their comprehensive teacher's guides and stay on-track with a tried-and-true curriculum that exceeds state standards. Other curriculum such as Bob Jones (BJU) and Alpha Omega (AOP) are also good choices but I prefer Abeka's presentation of the materials. In my opinion, Abeka is more engaging and less textbook-ish. (The ones above are Christian homeschool curriculum, non-religious equivalents would be Calvert Homeschool, BookShark or Timberdoodle.)

2. What are your goals for your homeschool and for your children?

I<small>F YOUR FIRST</small> *goal is to detox them from a stressful school environment and Zoom school meltdowns, then a more relaxed, family-centered approach may meet your needs for this year. Two curriculum providers that offer that type of product are Sonlight or My Father's World. (Non-religious options are GuidepostMontessori.com or Timberdoodle.)*

3. How old are your children?

. . .

Do you have a very advanced 3-year-old who needs to be challenged? Then maybe a more traditional approach would be appropriate. Do you have a 7-year-old with ADHD? Then a more physically demanding, hands-on approach would be the answer. Do you have a middle school or high school-aged child? Then maybe a more independent curriculum would work. There are some curriculum providers that I love but wouldn't recommend for high school. There are others I love for high school, but I don't like their elementary grade materials. You will need to spend some time looking over different curriculum to find what stands out to you. This includes looking inside the books to see how the information is presented and reading reviews. You will know when it's the right one when you love the curriculum too!

4. What is your home and work life like?

IF YOU CONTINUE to work while homeschooling, that changes the curriculum you choose. Do you have six kids and a newborn? Then a curriculum with subjects that can be taught together for all ages, with independent math books, might be a good choice. (See Jessica's school day.)

FOR THE PARENT'S first year, the curriculum they choose should be easy to implement, since the parent is learning more about homeschooling and investigating how their children learn.

Many people think that the "complete curriculum" books you find at Costco, Walmart or in bookstores are curriculum. They are not. The word curriculum refers to the lessons and the content that is taught in a particular course or program.

Curriculum is very subjective. Parents should pick one that they love and that their kids enjoy.

It doesn't matter if it's the best math program out there. If the parent hates it and dreads the very thought of pulling it out each day, then it's not the right one for their family.

If they are excited because the parent found one that they understand and can't wait to use it with the kids, then their enthusiasm will be contagious!

If the kids hate it and every day crying begins as soon as it's pulled out, then it may not be the right one.

However, if your child hates everything and cries about all of it, that's a character training problem, not a curriculum problem.

If parents are unhappy with the curriculum they have, see if they can tweak it to make it work.

If the workbook is black and white, tell the parent to take an evening and add stickers and highlights to the page to brighten it up. If it's not going deep enough, encourage the parent to find some manipulatives to add and some videos to go deeper. If it's got too much repetition, advise them to go through the book and cross out sections their child already knows and doesn't need any practice on.

I recommend finishing what they start. There are exceptions but encourage them to try to finish the curriculum this year and if necessary, make different choices next year.

You may also hear the term "eclectic homeschooling" which means that parents don't use one curriculum for all the subjects, they use different methods for each subject.

Parents who are new to homeschooling may not have noticed that there are some subjects their child does well and others where they struggle. Each year our family has a focus. If a child struggles in language arts then parents can focus this coming year on language arts and get a language program that is comprehensive.

When they do this, they might choose to go light with science and history by just reading through the books together. That way there is more time and energy to devote to language arts.

The next year that family can choose to focus on science and get a program that has a lot of science experiments. Balance comes over time, from adding all the years together. When people make mistakes in one direction, they can make corrections and go in the opposite direction the following year.

Going 110% on each subject can lead to lots of frustration for everyone.

Each year, we have one or two subjects we focus on.

Here are some examples of this for early elementary.

Kindergarten's focus would be on language and math. We would still do science and history, but they would just be something I read to that child on the couch, no workbook or testing.

First grade's focus would continue to be language and math and if I noticed that my child was having trouble with reading or math, I would take more time with one of those. We would continue to read through history and science together.

Second grade's focus again continues to be language and math, but science would have some more hands-on time with experiments like making slime or oobleck, field trips to the zoo or walks in nature observing what we were learning about in our textbook. Taking a magnifying glass into the yard, making pipe cleaner models of the inside of flowers. History might include longer discussions about our history textbook, field trips to museums and watching the *Liberty's Kids* series.

Third grade will look a lot like second grade except that the books will be longer, the words more complex and the concepts will take longer to teach and understand.

Workbooks are good for reinforcing what kids have been taught. They are for practicing and reviewing topics. Workbooks are not *for* teaching kids. Make sure parents don't just buy a workbook for math. Kids need a full math program for instruction. Unless the parent enjoys teaching math and sitting next to their children as they work on math, I would recommend getting video instruction for mathematics. Good choices for this are Math-U-See, Dive into Math, Abeka Academy and Teaching Textbooks.

. . .

PARENT EXERCISE

Find somewhere to be alone for an hour with a pen and paper. Think about each of your children:

1. How does that child learn best? (Is it by reading, hands-on activities, listening to audiobooks, through songs, in group classes, by watching a video?)
2. Thinking back on the past year, how has that child understood each subject? (Really grasped it, had difficulty with it, excelled at it, loved it, hated it, seems a year behind, needs a refresher, didn't grasp basic parts of it, could use the same level or grade but by a different curriculum to reinforce the concepts, needs someone who loves it as much as they do to teach it.)
3. What worked and what didn't work?
4. Which curriculum/program/method did I like or dislike? Why?
5. What does my child need? (A curriculum with songs on cd or a video or something interactive or a particular subject taught by someone else? Would they like more quizzes because they love to test themselves or would they like a class with peers because they love to work as a group?)
6. What does this child need to learn to be a successful, independent, adult?
7. I may not enjoy teaching (name a subject) _____ but it's important

for my child's future that they be able to

_____

(communicate effectively, write complete sentences, understand the natural world, have a good grasp of history, think critically, logically decipher information for truth and accuracy, be mathematically competent so they aren't cheated at the store/on taxes/during employment.) Without this skill, my child will be at a disadvantage in the world as an adult.

8. Looking at #2, which subjects do I need to incorporate into school to accomplish that goal?
9. How do I need to break up that information to get it completed by the time my child graduates from high school? *Are you putting off teaching English until the 12th grade? If so, can they learn all of that and really understand it in one year or would it be better to introduce it slowly, over time, so they can absorb it and make it part of how they write naturally? Can health be skipped as a "subject" each year and just be taught officially at 8th grade to cover anything you've missed in normal conversation over the years?*
10. Which curriculum/program/book/methods do I think will work best to accomplish each subject I want to teach this year?

"You can't hit a target you aren't aiming for."
-Zig Ziglar

Are Homeschool Kids in the Same Grade Level as Public School?

MANY PARENTS FIND that kids brought home from public school were not taught the basics. They may find that taking their sixth grader out of public school and putting her into a sixth grade homeschool curriculum may not work. She may not have the foundation required for understanding 6th grade homeschool curriculum. Another thing they may encounter is that she may have been doing pre-algebra in school (pre-algebra generally means a review of everything prior to algebra and introduces some algebra terms) so looking at sixth grade homeschool math that isn't labeled pre-algebra may make them think she's farther ahead than homeschool kids. But as they continue through the school year, they may notice that she's struggling with even the simplest of concepts. Yes, the school said she was at a certain math level, but she may have been rushed through it and never really understood it.

In homeschool we teach for mastery. If our kids don't get a concept, we stop and find another way to explain it. We search YouTube or we might realize that our child isn't mature enough to grasp that concept. In that case, we can stop and decide how to proceed. An example of this might be a child having difficulty with long division.

As you work with your child, you realize he doesn't

understand how division works, but more than that, he doesn't understand how multiplication works.

Now you must decide what to do.

Do you keep moving forward, knowing that what you're saying sounds like Charlie Brown's teacher? Or do you:

- Take a break from math for a day or two to see if he gets it in a few days?
- Stop and go backward, choosing to print out some multiplication worksheets and do those for several days?
- Spend a week listening to multiplication songs and doing multiplication problems until multiplication comes naturally?
- Print out some super simple division problems?

After that, you could return to the original math lesson with this new knowledge and confidence.

This is homeschooling.

One of the cool things I learned a long time ago is that 8th grade is a review year. Kids basically review everything they've learned in K-7th grade, to prepare for high school. Knowing this gives both you and the parents options.

Should Parents Buy New or Used Books?

Here are some guidelines to help parents who ask you decide which to purchase. If they're only reading through a subject, then used books are great. An example of this is that they're going to focus on language arts this year, that's the main priority. They also want to cover history, but not as in-depth as language arts. Maybe they will read history on the couch with all the children. History would then be the perfect subject to buy used. Why? Because they can pay pennies for items they just want to read through once. They don't care if another family highlighted parts of the book or answered the chapter questions in pencil and then erased them. They're just going through the subject to give the kids a general overview of it. If you're doing this, I recommend Abeka's history books for grades pre-K through 4th grade. The stories in them will engage all ages, including adults.

If they are using funds for other things then the subjects they are just reading through are the perfect places to do save money.

What can you find used?

There are people who begin to homeschool and then change their mind after two weeks or order curriculum and then hear about a local class and use that instead. These people will often have their books, tests, quizzes, and teacher's guides for sale as complete, unused sets on eBay. Other families know they are homeschooling for the long haul and have their kids take care of their books and write answers down in notebooks instead of in the workbook or book. Then they sell the like-new set on eBay for a little extra money.

If they're buying a used teacher's guide or answer key, encourage them to verify the exact edition number on all the books. For example, if they buy the *Saxon 6/5 Second*

Edition math book, the only answer key that will go with the correct lessons and problems is the *Saxon 6/5 Second Edition Answer Key*. The Saxon 6/5 first edition or third edition will almost never line up with the other editions. This is very important to know and verify before purchasing the student book and the teacher book separately. For first editions there isn't always something that names them as first editions on the front of the book or on the copyright page, but they can go to the copyright page and look at the year the book was published and verify they were published in the same year. Occasionally they may find a curriculum where the second edition book only has very minor changes, like pictures updated or pages laid out better, but usually the book and answer keys are not compatible.

When they buy something that doesn't need an answer key, like readers, then buying used is a great option! If they buy really used or really old books, this can save hundreds of dollars. For example, if a science book costs $29 new, but they can find the 1980s version of the book on eBay for $1.25 and buy one for each grade level for seven children, they would save $194.25.

Parents can find these older editions on eBay, on used homeschool book websites, at used book sales, at library book sales, at garage sales, in thrift stores, for free in giveaway piles, on Craigslist or on Facebook marketplace. This way they can spend their funds for field trips or classes.

"Readers" are especially great to buy used or old. The

term "readers" means the non-textbooks kids are supposed to read. Older kids would just read these to themselves. In the elementary grades, they would read them aloud to the parents. There are often questions at the end of the chapters (as there are in history and science books) but those are designed to be used in a classroom. The teacher needs to verify that the students have read the material and have understood what they read. Parents already know that their child has read the chapter, so they don't need these questions. I usually just ask my children to tell me about what they've read.

"Mom, I read chapter one."

"Great! What was it about?"

"Well, there was this dog and he got lost so the people were trying to find him, but..."

For history or science, parents can have them read the comprehension questions aloud while the parent is doing the dishes.

"Question one is who is Genghis Khan?"

"Great, who was he?"

"He led the Mongol Empire."

"Terrific."

"Question two is where was the Mongol Empire located? I don't know."

Parents can tell them to look back on what they've read and find it, then read out the answer. It's not something parents need to grade or stress over, it's just a review of the material they've covered. What's important is that they covered the material and that they understood it.

Textbooks are just convenient groupings of things people think each grade should know. They are there for ease of use, they aren't the end-all-be-all.

I like to vary the subjects that we use textbooks with each year.

Some years we need textbooks or workbooks for subjects I want my children to learn, but I don't have any passion for. Some years are just survival years (a new baby, health issues, etc.) Some years we are hitting one or two subjects hard and I just want a textbook for another subject that we will read and not delve into.

But the beauty of learning is to be immersed in a subject and see how it relates to real life.

A great way to introduce the study of history is to pick one point in time to concentrate on. To accomplish this, I chose a video game I grew up with, *The Oregon Trail*. It's available now as a retro handheld game. The object of *The Oregon Trail* is to make it from Independence, Missouri, to Oregon City, Oregon. To play the game, you have to budget your money, buy enough supplies to survive, hunt for food and barter with people along the way. Your kids think it's just a game, but they will learn history, use math skills and become familiar with United States geography.

Using this game allows parents to pinpoint a particular point in "the olden days" and when you learn about the Pilgrims, you can say, "The Pilgrims were before the Oregon Trail." When you learn about the civil rights movement, you can say, "This was after the Oregon Trail." Having a specific point in time gives kids a solid frame of reference. They could even make a timeline to help illustrate this.

When the family visits a museum, they will see things that relate to the Oregon Trail time period and can explain that to the children. Get books at the library about the Oregon Trail. Make time to watch documentaries about the Oregon Trail and check out books about the famous trail guides and landmarks along the way.

A similar retro handheld game is *Where in the World is Carmen Sandiego*. This game takes children around the globe as they try to find stolen artifacts. I have fond memories of my siblings and I gathered around our Commodore 64 computer with notebooks and encyclopedias and an atlas as we tried to figure out the clues.

Tips to Give Parents to Make Homeschooling Easier

1. Make freezer meals or buy frozen meals for your first week of school. Inevitably, your husband will walk in the door, and you'll be shocked that the whole day has passed and you haven't even thought of dinner. That's because for the first week we're not sure how long each subject is going to take and don't have a real schedule yet.
2. Prioritize social events like weekly park days. Social events will be the first things that you'll

want to let go of when you're feeling overwhelmed or behind. But they are the best for giving all of you a refreshing break and for helping you cope.

3. Start strong! A lot of families like to ease into the subjects. For our family that was counterproductive. The first few months of school have always been our most productive. Those are the days when we are the most excited. We have new books, new classes, new smells, new pencils, and new enthusiasm for school. We jump in with both feet and do every subject, knowing that by the end of the school year I'll be yelling, "Just do math and language, and call it a day!"

4. Warn your husband that the first week is going to be hard and that you'll need his patience when nothing else gets done. No laundry, dishes or yard work will get done on time.

5. After your first week, give yourself a little reward, like going for a walk with a friend, reading a good book or some time alone.

6. Do your own version of meal prep or cook 3-4 pounds of ground beef over the weekend, then divide it up into zip top freezer bags and stick them in the freezer. If you find out it's dinnertime and you didn't plan anything you can grab one of these frozen ground beef bags and throw it into spaghetti sauce, microwave it

for tacos, make hamburger macaroni and cheese, have beef stew, put it in ramen noodles with some frozen veggies, or have quick nachos. You can also make hamburger patties ahead of time and freeze them along with hamburger buns for quick meals. Try cutting up fruits and vegetables over the weekend for salads, snacks, and quick stews. You can also find crock pot meals to start in the morning before school and overnight oatmeal recipes for breakfasts.
7. Make a school supply shopping list at the beginning of each school year and load up on the supplies you and the kids need at the cheapest prices they will be all year. Even if they don't really need anything, it will help them get excited about the new school year.

I don't want to teach my children that they get a prize for everything they do in life, however it is nice for them to have a little happy moment for schoolwork that is well done.

The system that has worked for us is:

- On tests, get an A, visit the prize box
- On tests, get a B, earn a scratch-n-sniff sticker
- On daily work, get an A, earn a sticker

My kids *love* taking tests so they can visit the prize box. Our prize box has inexpensive things like fancy pens, fun erasers, dollar store items, treats, and sometimes a higher-priced item like a book.

Are There any Curriculums You Recommend?

Yes. I prefer to use a curriculum that has been around for a while and has shown excellent results. These are a few I can recommend, but Mary Pride's website and books will give you many more options. I have a link to her website at NinaHelpsYouHomeschool.com.

There is a quick way to get started with very little stress or shopping around. It will give parents time to learn more about homeschooling and explore their options while the child is still learning, it is to start with Abeka Academy's unaccredited independent study.

Abeka is quite rigorous and as you'll see in the sample consult at the end of the book, there are particular ways I recommend using it. It is also one of the curriculum providers that I would not necessarily recommend in its entirety for older grades. When parents buy it for preschool through third grade, the workload is manageable. This allows the children to still have plenty of outdoor time. However, the workload takes longer and becomes more difficult as the grades go up. This is perfect for families who prefer a rigorous educational program for their children.

Those who would like more time in junior high or high school for out of the home activities can easily continue with Abeka Academy by simply choosing their individual subject option or purchasing the entire year but only doing certain subjects.

The Abeka Academy teachers are extremely skilled at video instruction and since Abeka has been used by homeschooling families and elite Christian schools for so long, their methods are excellent. In the video instruction, the teacher will ask questions of the class and then turn to the camera and say, "Now students watching, you answer this question." Then they pause for an answer and have one student in the classroom answer.

The beauty of parents using this program their first year is that they will learn how to schedule and teach their children with plenty of help and modeling. They will hear and see how Abeka uses its materials and how they structure the school day. Then the next year they can buy just the student and teacher books from Abeka and teach the children themselves. In their third homeschool year, they can pick from a variety of curriculums. By then parents will have a better understanding of how each of their children learns and where they excel or struggle. Abeka academy also comes with your daily lesson plan to tell exactly what the child is going to do that day. (Calvert Homeschool would be the non-religious version of this.)

Abeka's video option is also great for:

- Teaching a subject that parents don't want to teach

- An older child to do one or two subjects alone, as the parent teaches younger children
- Help when the parent can't teach or if they work during the day

For math the first year, Teaching Textbooks is a good option. This is a math program that teaches and grades everything for you. This happens automatically and is online. They also make a paper version.

We used this for a year and a half with my youngest, while we were focusing on other subjects.

It was great the first year we used it. By the middle of the second year, it wasn't working anymore. The concepts were too abstract to sink in through online learning. When you type something into a computer, it's not the same thing as writing it down with pen and paper. There are different neural pathways in the brain that are formed when you write something down.

If a child is a wiz at math, then he or she could use Teaching Textbooks and just move forward at a faster pace or start in a grade above. It was a great fit for us the first year we used it, but not the second, so your results may vary. I like it for first year homeschoolers because it will ease them into the homeschool routine and help them see where their child is in math.

For those who feel like they learned nothing in school or that they don't see the importance of teaching language arts, remind those parents that we have already had this teaching. We can talk about the necessity of teaching these subjects because we have already learned how to read and write. Failing to teach our children the fundamentals is failing to teach them the very things that will help them excel. They may choose not to further their education. They may choose to work for themselves, in this case understanding math and how to communicate will be essential. They may choose to be garbage handlers or groundskeepers, but if parents don't provide them with the skills to add up their paychecks or write a proper email to a customer, then they're setting them up for failure.

Some of the best homeschool resources will seem old-fashioned or uncool at first. They may turn parents off, but over time they will become heartwarming favorites with familiar faces.

You've heard me mention several of the curriculum options below. These are ones I think are worth knowing about to see if they are a good fit for your families. There is additional information at NinaHelpsYouHomeschool.com. There are also many review videos on YouTube. Just type in the curriculum's name and the word "review" for example, "Teaching Textbooks review."

- Apologia
- Master Books
- Drive Thru Menu Math
- Alpha Omega (AOP)
- The Critical Thinking Company
- Saxon Math (preferably 1st and 2nd editions, but new editions are fine)

- Story of the World (books, audiobooks, and activity books)
- Handwriting Without Tears (HWT)
- Times Tales
- Challenge Math by Edward Zaccaro
- Common Sense Science
- Learning Language Arts Through Literature (LLATL)
- Mystery of History (MOH)
- Institute for Excellence in Writing (IEW)
- Math-u-See (MUS)
- Sonlight

Vicki Says:

Does your student know what the agenda is for the day, and what "finished for today" looks like? Would you be motivated to work diligently if it felt as though every time you finished something, someone just gave you another assignment? There's not much incentive to get finished, is there? Our kids' days can feel daunting—or even unending.

So, it was important to me that my kids see the lesson plan, that they know what the expectation was for the day, to help me evaluate if it was reasonable, and that there was an ending point each day for my demands on their attention.

While I was writing this (on a deadline, of course), I time-chunked some blocks of time to hunker down and hammer it out. This is how my "sit down and work on your assignment" time worked out.

- I did two loads of laundry.
- I updated the photo gallery on my website.
- I made a batch of cookies.
- I checked work e-mails.
- I made travel arrangements for an upcoming speaking engagement.

If there were a tactful way to put a "shaking my head" emoji into a book, this is where it would go!

Maybe it was my highly distractible brain kicking in, or maybe it was just too much to handle in one (or five) sittings, and I needed to break it up, accomplish some other tasks that were on my mind, or let my brain process in between paragraphs.

It's possible that this is how our kids are as soon as we ask them to sit still and work on something for what feels like ages to them. Our kids are people. And sometimes that dawdling kiddo isn't being rebellious or lazy or slow. Sometimes he's just distracted, or he's on overload and needs a brain break.

Remember the old adage *you can lead a horse to water but you can't make him drink?* That may be so, but I propose that the corollary to that statement is: *But you sure can salt his oats!*

So... I *"salted my own oats"* with the knowledge that I'd feel good when I'd gotten my thoughts organized on paper. I made sure it was a task that I was *mature enough in my abilities* to handle. I gave myself *choices* in how and when I wrote. I internalized a *plan and expectations*. I made it *relevant* to my passion for encouraging homeschoolers. And I drew on my *connection* to Nina—my friend—and thus aspired to honor and respect her by getting this to her in a timely manner.

And the now-thirsty proverbial horse drank the water.

Extra Information

There are free homeschool programs such as AmblesideOnline, Easy Peasy All-in-One Homeschool, and The Good and the Beautiful. I have not used any of these so I cannot speak about them knowledgably.

All families make tremendous sacrifices in order to homeschool their children. Families for whom money is tight are choosing their children's future over making more money for the household. I admire and respect these families for the strength they show. Their children have a chance at a better future with a far better education than the public school can provide.

Middle-income families have the option to look at more

expensive curriculum and use the payment plan options that most of them provide. The education they are providing is equivalent to a private school education for a fraction of the cost.

Higher income families make the sacrifice in perception. They may feel that peers will look down on their choice, but who said that sending children to private school was the best option? The same issues in public school happen in the private schools. There is also the added strain of families whose children they have kicked out of public schools. These families pay to have the school keep their out-of-control child in school at the expense of the teacher's ability to teach and the other children's safety and ability to learn.

Chapter 5

Should the House Look Like a School?

How do Parents Create a Learning Environment?

Some homeschoolers tell new families not to "school at home." What they are saying is don't attempt to model a typical school day at home.

Often new homeschoolers create a schoolroom in their house with desks, a flag and a chalkboard or whiteboard. They use their memories from elementary school classrooms to create a fun learning environment for their children.

While this is a fun and creative idea, it's unnecessary and many long-term homeschooling parents don't find this situation sustainable. Why? Because five hours into the hardest homeschool day, mom still won't be able to leave the schoolroom to cook dinner or do a load of laundry.

Most of us "do school" all around the house. It's great to have a desk, crates or storage closet to keep all their school stuff in, but having a set area for school isn't usually necessary.

Families work together at the kitchen table or on the couch or on the floor. We just need a place to hold books, workbooks and supplies.

We've had desks for each of our kids, we've had a group table, we've had bins, now that I only have one child left at home, we use two crates to hold all our school materials for the year.

You can encourage parents to make learning zones in the house, like workstations. One zone is the computer, facing the rest of the house, so parents can watch what the children are doing on the computer at all times. They can send the children to the couch or on the living room carpet or to lie down with the dog and curl up with a blanket while they read their history textbook or daily reading books. We use the kitchen bar area for art or reading a science book as I cook dinner. Parents can send kids to lie on their beds while they draw for art class. Some use the kitchen table for math. It's not unusual to see kids reading upside down in their tree fort or coloring their anatomy workbook outside in the grass.

Kids with more sensory needs will enjoy reading while on a swing or shouting math facts while jumping on a mini trampoline.

Some days, I cut up all the math problems and hide them around the house. The kids have to find each problem, complete it and find the next one.

Part of creating a learning environment may be to remove electronics until after 4pm or only on the weekends. It may also include removing streaming services or apps.

As parents feel more empowered in their roles as homeschool teachers, they will see educational opportunities everywhere. One year we heard about the movie *Sergeant York*, a terrific movie that is a true story. Since the movie takes place during World War I, my son and I started learning about World War I. We visited museums and veteran centers. He dug a trench in the backyard and had fake battles with his friends. They watched the movie together. We took out maps and found the places where the battles took place, and we bought the World War I Map Game by Learningames and played it until we had all the places memorized. Thinking back on that year is a fun memory, and it was a great year of learning for us both.

For some subjects, like geography, parents can use a game instead of a textbook. Instead of flash cards or drills, math games and history games are great reinforcement for what your kids have just learned.

In *The Read-Aloud Handbook,* author Jim Trelease recommends allowing kids to read below their reading level when they are reading for pleasure. He says the ease of reading below their reading level can cultivate a love of reading in children who don't always enjoy it.

I got sneaky with this and put lower-level reading books in places where my kids would be bored like in the car, in the bathroom or at the kitchen table. If I place a book in these places and don't mention it, they will usually pick it up and start reading it on their own.

This won't work, however, if children have entertainment at their fingertips with a phone, tablet, video game or computer. Kids need to be bored in order to start thinking outside the box. They need to lie on the grass and look up at cloud shapes with friends and dig in the dirt looking for worms. They need to stare at the wall and make shapes or faces out of textured walls. This is how we got our great music, from bored people hearing songs in their heads. I'm sure we've all seen the meme asking how many talented musicians, artists, inventors, and scientists have never existed because kids were never bored long enough to create.

We don't want to deprive children of being bored. It's in our boredom that ideas for books and inventions come.

The other day, a mom asked our Facebook group how we get everything accomplished. The answer is, we don't. One day, the house is clean, but we only got through half our subjects. The next day, the school day is fantastic, but the house looks like it was robbed. Something has to give. Parents are rarely going to have everything go perfectly.

Years ago, I learned to put the house back together 30 minutes before my husband came home from work. Trying to clean throughout the day just left me exhausted, and the house was a mess by the time he came home.

If I have dinner ready and the house is in good shape after a day of school, I feel like I'm queen of the world. The tips I gave in chapter 4 will help parents get a better handle on this. If parents picture themselves as jugglers with ten balls in the air, they can imagine that every day at least one ball is going to drop. The nice thing is that once they get a good rhythm, they'll drop fewer balls each day. Encourage parents to keep picking them up and starting again.

Are There Community Resources for Homeschoolers?

It may take several months to find the resources in your community, but most cities have group classes for homeschoolers. An example of this might be an art class put on by your local art or pottery studio. Your local makers' club might have a robotics class for homeschoolers. Churches may have their classrooms rented out for homeschool classes or co-ops. Piano teachers often have homeschool group classes or lessons during the day. Stables offer homeschool riding lessons and classes. It's just a matter of finding each of these.

Another way to find these is to ask the people who run each business if they have a homeschool group class. If they like the idea, they may ask you to spread the word and see if you can get enough interest to offer a class.

What is a Homeschool Convention?

How do I know all these things about homeschooling? Well, it's because I'm the smartest woman on the planet. Oh wait, no it isn't. The truth is, I've been to many years of homeschool conventions. Just like teachers have in-service days for professional development, homeschool parents do as well, it's called the homeschool convention.

Each summer there is a homeschool convention in every area of the country. At these events, they fill an entire auditorium with hundreds of homeschool curriculum vendors who can answer questions, let parents touch and flip through things, and chat with any kids.

There are also famous keynote speakers. There are also smaller rooms with speakers on topics such as "how to homeschool your special needs child," "incorporating art into your homeschool," "the Montessori method," and "helping your right-brain learner understand math."

It's important for parents to attend one of these as soon

as possible. They will give them encouragement and insight as they gather with thousands of homeschool parents.

You may think it's crazy to hear a homeschooling mom rave about a math curriculum, but once they've been to a homeschool convention and heard a speaker explain something that has confused them for years, they won't be able to stop raving.

For the years that they can't make it to the convention, good homeschool magazine subscriptions like *The Old Schoolhouse* give a lot of great information.

Chapter 6

How Can Parents Make Sure Homeschool is Successful?

We are not raising children, we are raising adults.

Think about the statement above. In homeschooling the goal is not to raise large children who, at age 18, are trying to figure out how to be adults. The goal is to slowly and steadily turn an infant into a prepared and successful adult. That is the goal.

Are You Saying You Run Your Home Like a Business?

Yes. I run my home like I'm running a company. I make file folders for bills, schoolwork I want to save, official documents, medical information and so forth.

Encourage parents to have a binder with tabs to keep answer keys they pull out from the back of a workbook, printables they find online, a record of what each child has done that day and any lesson plans of what they hope to accomplish and when. A binder is also a great place to store any homeschool articles they like.

Here is an example of a family with kids aged 10, 5, and 3:

John- Science: p. 5-8
    Math: lesson 8
    Reading: "Charlotte's Web" chapter 2
    Grammar: lesson 8
    Spelling: list 1 review
    History: chapter 2

Sally- Language: p.3
    Math: p.3
    Science: p.5-8

Ben- Dollar store workbook page
    Build with blocks

When homeschooling for the long term,
the thing about homeschooling is,
if they mess up one year,
They can fix it the next.

WHEN PARENTS HOMESCHOOL for the short term, the pressure to keep up with the school system, will weigh heavily on them. It will affect how they choose curriculum and how hard they push their kids. This leads to a lot of excess stress. It does not lead to effective homeschooling.

I fluctuate one way or the other. One year I push hard for academic excellence, making formal education the top priority. At the end of that year, I realize that we've not done enough hands-on activities, field trips or group activities. So, the next year we do all the things we missed the previous year and I lighten up on the academics. At the end of that year, I realize we didn't go as in-depth into some subjects as I would have liked, so the next year we hit it hard and back and forth. The beauty of it is that I can course correct immediately. Did we join too many sports teams and are running around all over the place this year? Next year, we will commit to only one. Did we skip the Christmas or Valentine's Day party? We will make those events next year.

Balance comes when we put all the years together. It doesn't always happen in the moment. Parents are going to make mistakes. That's normal. But hopefully the mistakes they make will not be from lack of love for their children.

Encourage them not to neglect going to events, they need the community support even more than their kids do.

Remind parents: You're not trying to convince your children to love homeschooling. It will feel like it sometimes, but that's not your actual goal. You decided to homeschool because of the reasons you wrote down at the beginning of this book. Children make poor decisions regularly, like not bathing, wanting to eat candy for every meal or wanting to play in the street. The reasons you decided to homeschool have nothing to do with what your children want at that particular moment. If your son comes crying to you because he misses his friends and wants to go back to school, that is a hint that you need to find more social activities for him.

How Can Parents Know if They're Doing it Right?

At first they won't know. They will just be getting used to everything and so will the kids. What you're looking for during the first six months is a change in attitude. Are the kids getting the routine down? Are they relaxing and feeling more comfortable in their own skin? Are they making friends? Are they learning to read for pleasure and getting to know the library?

Eventually you will be able to measure progress by seeing that in the beginning the child struggled with 1+1 and now they are doing 12+12 easily.

Over the past 17 years, I've watched hundreds of

families pull their children out of school and begin homeschooling. When their child attends their first park day, they are often withdrawn and wearing clothing that was more of a protective shield in school. It's not unusual to see girls dressed in black or thick clothing on their first park day, but within a few months they are wearing pastel colors, laughing, and smiling. Seeing the tear-filled eyes of their parents as they watch their child turn back into themselves is awe-inspiring.

You can also watch for new skills that the children develop. When they had limited time at home, did they learn how to cook? Now that they're home all day, parents can make sure they learn how to make simple meals like quesadillas, spaghetti, scrambled eggs, macaroni and cheese, grilled cheese sandwiches, tacos, and baked potatoes. For a young child, reading a recipe could count as reading for the day. Following directions is an important skill to master and measuring ingredients is the practical application of the math skills they are learning.

What Can Parents do While Waiting for Materials to Arrive?

Until the books arrive, families can go on field trips and there are excellent websites such as TeachersPayTeachers.com with thousands of printable activities to go with those field trips.

They can take a trip to the zoo and search online for "free zoo worksheet 6 grade" and print off something for each child to do following their zoo trip. The following day, they could head to the library and have each child get a book on the animal they liked the best. Parents could expand this into finding an Animal Planet program on this animal or an area of the world such as "animals of the tropics" or "nocturnal animals."

This would also be a great time to recreate some of the parent's favorite memories from childhood, like making a diorama or creating a vinegar and baking soda volcano.

What is Deschooling?

Some children need to come down from the stress or trauma they encountered at school and "de-school" for the first 2-4 weeks. If so then a de-schooling routine might look like:

- Taking field trips
- Watching educational documentaries
- Assigning a research project
- Getting to know the library
- Visiting homeschool events, classes, and co-ops
- Reading The Tuttle Twins book series
- Watching the entire series of *Engineering an Empire, Liberty's Kids,* and *Drive Through History*

Vicki Says:

You may have heard the term *de-schooling* (this is not the same as *un-schooling*, which is a teaching approach—but some unschooling tips also work for de-schooling[8]). *De-schooling* refers to taking a period of time to allow your child to rediscover the wonder of learning. As explained in "Suddenly Homeschooling: The Basics,"[9]

"De-schooling is a fancy term for letting go of the old paradigm and realizing that homeschooling doesn't have to look like school at home. It may take a month or more to adjust to the idea of *facilitating your child's learning*, vs *schooling* him.

It's okay to let your kids de-school by simply reading, or learning about something they want to learn about, or taking some virtual field trips, or working on a hobby, or cooking with you, or doing a family project.

(Translation: Learning can still happen just in the context of being a family–so enjoy!)"

Remember that this is a transition for your child, too—not just academically, but socially and emotionally as well. His familiar routine—his security—has changed. Be patient with your child, and remember that this is new for him, too. He may not know how to handle the freedom; he may need you to guide him in what to do, and work gradually into more self-direction.

De-schooling is also an opportunity for you to rediscover the wonder of your family! When I consult with families, I try to help them get a sense of what their family vision is and what sorts of activities they enjoy, so we can endeavor to find a homeschool approach that's a good fit for who they are as a family. And when that happens, children are more likely to be willing participants in the learning process.

Chapter 7

Are Homeschooled Kids Socialized?

Are Homeschoolers Uncool?

At first homeschool kids don't seem cool because they don't feel pressured to keep up with the latest trends or wear much makeup. Studies have shown that homeschoolers tend to have better interactions between age groups[16], so they are less likely to exclude new kids.

Newly homeschooled middle and high school kids are often stunted in interpersonal relationship building because of the public-school environment where walking up to a new person or group of kids doesn't go well at school.

For kids who have been homeschooled for several years, there is a stark difference. When new homeschoolers come to an event, I usually grab a child I know and ask them to introduce the new kid. They are happy to do it. I say, "Janice, this is Erica. She's new to the group. Would you mind introducing her to the other girls?"

99% of the time this goes very well and the new child feels welcomed. The time or two when this hasn't happened it's usually because the new child will not interact with the other kids and alienates them. This can go away with time. They are just scared.

The homeschool environment is so different that generally by the next school year that new homeschooler is the one I ask to introduce another new person. It will feel like the first day at a new school or the first day at a new job. Parents usually hate it, but encourage them to keep attending.

Parents can get over this uncomfortable feeling by going to the same events each week. If there is a weekly park date encourage them to go to it rain or shine, even when the kids don't want to go. Persistence will pay off. The first 5-6 times the children may not leave their parent's side. They may refuse to talk with anyone, but at some point something unplanned will happen.

It could be that the pouty teen drops her art supplies and another girl her age helps picks them up and says she also likes to draw manga characters. Or a pre-teen brings his skateboard and suddenly finds himself surrounded by eager little faces saying how cool his flips are. It only takes one good interaction for the feelings to change. It's a process, but if families persevere there can be a good outcome.

If They Build it, Will They Come?

If parents can't find the classes or activities they are looking for, encourage them to set them up! There are several ideas below.

Playgroups
Co-ops
Classes
Field trips
Park days
Mom's night out
Holiday parties
Cooking classes
Animal care
Gardening
Farm skills
Zoo field trip
Museums
Fast food or bakery or candy making tours
Planetarium
College tours
Hiking
Pottery
Painting
Scavenger hunt
Fruit picking
Woodworking
Food pantry

Factory
Recycling center
Fire station
Google "homeschool field trip ideas"

Chapter 8

Helping Parents Handle Hard Days

It's okay for parents to love what they're doing and still need a break.

Make sure to tell parents they will hyperventilate at least twice a year and wonder if they're ruining their kids! They will question their ability to teach. They will wonder if the kids are getting all the social time and educational opportunities that they need. They will question their sanity. But then they will have a moment the next week when they realize that this IS working and that it's the right thing to do.

If children struggle with a subject, as homeschoolers, parents can slow down to make sure the kids get it before moving on, just make sure the parents aren't setting the bar too low.

When my youngest struggled with math, I instituted a new prize system. Getting a 90% or higher on a math page would earn a visit to the prize box. To my surprise I found that the child who struggled in math could get an A when given a reason to focus. My child was more capable than I thought.

"Fool me once, shame on you. Fool me twice, shame on me."
-Italian Proverb

PARENT TIP:

How to Have a Happy Homeschool

Step #1- Stop trying to have a happy homeschool. That will put a lot of pressure on you. Homeschooling is like working out, cleaning your room, or eating your vegetables. It's not the fun part of life. You don't jump out of bed and think, "Yay, I can't wait to clean my room!" But you're much happier in a clean room. Homeschooling can be fun, but that's not the main goal. Your goal is to raise adults with the skills necessary to be successful in this world.

Step #2- Remember WHY you decided to homeschool. You didn't decide to homeschool because you couldn't imagine five minutes without your children. You did it because _____.

Step #3- If you can't find it, create it. I've seen a lot of parents complain when some activity doesn't exist. If you can't find a group class that your child wants, create it yourself. That's how the classes currently offered began.

Step #4- Realize what the homeschool community is and isn't. We are fellow travelers on the same journey you're on. Community is giving and taking in turns. Make sure you're giving as much as you are taking.

Step #5- Have some perspective. When I was a kid, I hated meatloaf. Yuck. I sat for a long time after dinner staring at cold meatloaf that I didn't want to eat. But now I sometimes crave meatloaf and have very warm, nostalgic feelings when I eat it. What my parents were doing was creating a foundation of good eating that would disappear in my early adult life but reappear as foundational when I had a family of my own.

You're doing the same.

You're creating an environment of learning, family and the things that are important to you (health, self-expression, individuality, self-sufficiency, independence, creativity.) While they may not jump out of bed excited to learn, you are giving them a foundation they will return to at some point.

Step #6- Stop comparing your worst day/week/year to someone's best moment. That happy homeschool family, with the matching hand-sewn outfits and their hand-ground wheat to make homemade bread, isn't perfect. They would probably tell you that if you asked. People post pictures and examples of their wins. They rarely post photos of the days when their kids are crying on the floor because they asked them to pick up a pencil.

This is a marathon. Some points are painful, but the results are worth it. Keep your eye on the prize!

How Can I Guide Parent who Homeschool Multiple Kids at the Same Time?

Encourage parents to post this question on their local homeschool Facebook group or asking moms at homeschool events for advice. This will give parents insight into how each family accomplishes this.

I can remember homeschooling in the hallway when our youngest was a toddler. Many families do this. They put the youngest child or two in their own room and put a baby gate across the door. Then the mom sits at the baby gate and teaches the other children who are laying or sitting in the hallway. This way, the toddler is contained, and the siblings can concentrate without a little sibling grabbing their paper or pencil.

Parents can also make use of a highchair and playpen during this age. Putting a toddler in their highchair and giving them toys or activities to play with while parents work with their older children works well. Clipping toys to the tray so they can't be thrown off is also helpful.

Take advantage of nap time. When toddlers wake up, parents can put on an educational program while the toddler is in the playpen if they need more time to work with older kids.

It's also a great idea to put away some toys and bring out different toys each week. This will help little kids be excited to play with them. Learning toys like Lincoln Logs, Legos, wooden blocks and wood puzzles are great items for young kids to use while parents are teaching. If parents pull out the Legos one week and then put those away and pull out the wooden blocks the next week, they'll have better luck keeping them occupied.

When parents teach multiple school-aged children, it's helpful to look for curriculum that is designed for multiple ages.

What About Parents With Children with Special Needs?

Parents can keep their child's IEP and still get services while homeschooling.

If a child is struggling or has special needs, Dianne Craft is the specialist to check out. Her resources are recommended by almost every homeschool convention. I've included a link to her website at NinaHelpsYou-Homeschool.com.

Her website has a free one-hour video where she covers Tourette's, dyslexia, dysgraphia, ADHD, behavioral issues, learning issues, trouble sitting still, language issues, balance issues, trouble with learning sight-words and raising gifted children.

Her video is a must-watch for every homeschooling parent.

There is also a company called Thinking Tree Books that makes the Fun-Schooling curriculum. These workbooks are great for moms with chronic illness, children with dyslexia or dysgraphia and things for kids to do when the teaching parent is sick.

The font in the books is made especially for kids with dyslexia and inside the books are things for the kids to do by themselves. You should look through these books to understand just how they work, so you can recommend them to parents.

Remind parents that the workbooks at the store labeled "comprehensive curriculum" are *not* homeschool curriculum. These are review or busywork. They don't actually teach the concepts.

How Can I Help Parents Who Feel Overwhelmed?

If parents get stuck and think they need to put your children back in school, encourage them to reach out to their local homeschool group. There is usually someone who is available to talk them off the edge. Homeschooling is tough work. I can't tell you how many times I've grabbed the phone and when my friend Sue answered the phone, instead of hearing "hello" all she heard was, "Talk me down!" We would each vent about our homeschool day and end up laughing. You might just be their "Sue."

It's not always easy, but it's always worth it. With this community around them, homeschooling parents are never alone, even when it feels like it.

I need "me time" that's why I get up at 5am every

weekday. That gives me two hours in the morning to myself. I also want "me time" in the evening. The way I explain it to my family is, "After 14 hours together, I need some alone time. After 8pm I'm tired and grumpy." Parents can also use the words, "After ___pm I can't be a good mom." This helps the family to understand that they need to let the teaching parent have their own time to decompress after being patient all day.

Parents can make that time whatever works for them. Some days it may be the moment the spouse walks in the door, other days it could be after 7pm.

It's a nice way to express that mommy needs to replenish her cup of patience and kindness.

This doesn't mean that the teaching parent doesn't love their family or that homeschooling is too much to handle. It just means that after a long day of being patient and kind, their cup is empty.

Once the family gets used to it, it will be easy to set this time aside. Parents can experiment and find out what this replenishing time looks like for them. It could be a bath, a book, an uninterrupted phone call with a friend, a walk, a movie, or sitting outside.

It's normal to feel overwhelmed sometimes.

It's normal to feel smothered sometimes.

It's normal to feel like they're failing sometimes.

It's okay to take some time to refill their cup.

If they need a break during the week and can't afford or find a class or group, they can find another homeschool mom and make a plan to swap kids for two hours a week. If there is something they love to do like teach art, make crafts, teach music or science, they offer to do that once a week with the other person's kids and then have the other person do what she loves once a week with theirs. Each parent will get a break.

Vicki Says:

I'll be honest. There are days I just don't feel like doing the dishes. I may balk at getting started. I may dread taking the time. But eventually common sense (or the idea of having to do two days' worth tomorrow!) wins, and I talk myself into doing the responsible thing and getting them done.

Some days, our kids are like that. It's just been a long day, or they are interested in something else right now, or they dread getting started. (This is a normal scenario on occasion in many homeschool settings. It really isn't just your kiddo!) But our hope is that eventually they will realize that putting it off now just makes it tougher later, so they buckle down and cooperate.

What if Their Child Can't Focus?

To have the best school day possible, encourage parents to make sure breakfast is high in protein and has no sugar or gluten. Sugar and gluten cause brain fog and sugar crashes. This is easy to do by making eggs with bacon.

Tell parents to keep a glass of water available all day to break a bad mood or help with concentration.

An example of this is when Billy breaks down over his fifth math problem and the parent repeats the problem to him through clenched teeth. They can quickly change the mood by changing tone and saying, "Oh, wait, you haven't had a drink of water yet. Go grab some."

Sometimes this simple trick of diverting attention away from the problem by getting Billy to move out of his seat will work. Having a cool drink of refreshing water to replenish his dehydrated brain and body will also help.

On hard days, I imagine I'm Batman and pretend I have a "focusing tool belt." I use the same tactic as with the water, but this time have the child get a piece of sugarless gum or trail mix, celery and peanut butter, carrots and dressing, string cheese or nuts. The final tool in the focusing tool belt is an essential oil roller, like doTERRA's "Motivation" blend. Again, I'll distract him with, "Oh, I know what we need, we forgot to use our motivation roller!"

Having these tools to pull out when things are tough is empowering for both parents and children. Kids probably don't even know why they are in such a grumpy mood.

Parents are helping them see that there are things they can do to snap out of a bad mood.

Parents can also set goals like, "two more problems and then we're going outside!" Or, "As soon as we finish math, we can head to the park."

What About Parents with an Only Child?

When families have one child at home, getting them out of the house to be with other kids is more important. Parents will have to prioritize this in ways that families with six kids don't need to. Those kids always have a playmate in the house.

While socialization isn't the primary concern of homeschool, it is a valid concern when families have an only child. If there are plenty of kids in the neighborhood that the child is already friends with, then they may not need to make the extra effort. If this is not the case, then they'll need to sign up for more field trips, more park days, and more activities so their child will have plenty of friends in the homeschool group. Even with after-school friends, an only child would benefit from having friends who are available during the day for last-minute activities.

Parents of only children must work harder at creating social time for their kids. That's the only real difference between homeschooling multiple children and homeschooling an only child.

What Should Parents Teach at Each Stage?

Lost Tools of Learning Chart

Grades K-2	Grades 3-7
Pre-Polly	**Poll-Parrot**
• Excited about learning • Enjoys playing games, hearing stories, songs and projects • Has a short attention span • Likes to copy & imitate • Needs to touch, smell, taste, feel, see • Is imaginative & creative	• Likes to explain and figure things out • Excited about new and interesting facts • Relates his own exeriences to the subject • Likes to collect and organize things • Likes to repeat rhymes & chants • A great time to learn a new language
How to Teach	**How to Teach**
• Explore & find things • Hands-on learning • Build, color, draw, sing, play games • Short, creative projects • Repeat stories back to you • Field trips • Give copying and imitating opportunities	• Make collections, displays & models • Lessons should weave through subjects & senses • Teach and assign simple projects • Drama, memorization, repeating, chants, songs • Drills & games • Oral presentations • Field trips

@2023 Nina Elena, adapted from Tom Garfield

Grades 7-9	Grades 10-12
Pert	**Poetic**
<ul><li>Likes to debate, judge, critique and is critical of things</li><li>Likes to show off his knowledge</li><li>Likes to organize things and people</li><li>Wants to know "why"</li><li>Thinks is smarter than adults</li><li>Excited but wants to be challenged</li><li>Likes "insider" knowledge</li></ul>	<ul><li>Idealistic</li><li>Interested in current events and his own life</li><li>Concerned with justice and fairness</li><li>Developing special interests/hobbies</li><li>Can work independently and take on responsibility</li><li>Expresses his own feelings & ideas</li></ul>
How to Teach	**What to Teach**
<ul><li>Debates & persuasive reports</li><li>Guest speakers & trips</li><li>Collaborative work in groups</li><li>Time lines, maps, charts & other visual material</li><li>Drama, role-play and reenactments of events</li><li>Evaluate & critique</li><li>Learn rules of logic</li><li>Research projects & presentations</li></ul>	<ul><li>Classic literature, history, speeches & debate</li><li>Write papers & discuss his worldview</li><li>Construct a public defense of a thesis</li><li>Expore drama & poetry & giving oral presentations</li><li>Learn how to research and present cohesive ideas</li><li>Added responsibilities</li><li>Field trips</li></ul>

Chapter 9

Is it Possible to Homeschool Well in High School?

Kids don't understand why it's happening, but they sense themselves being put to death in school. That's why they hate it so much. -John Taylor Gatto

What Challenges Does High School Present?

High school can be one of the most rewarding times to homeschool. Teens are beginning to venture into the world and are becoming adults. They have thoughts and opinions to share and will often amaze adults with their insights.

This is also a time when peer pressure in school is the most dangerous. It's not always pressure to do a particular thing, but pressure to disappear into the background. High schoolers feel like they have a giant target on their backs and one wrong move will bring unwanted attention from the crowd.

While hormones can make some high schoolers emotional, being there for their emotional and educational needs is important. They need a stable adult to discuss their plans with, a shoulder to cry on and help them navigate working outside the home.

One way to engage high school children and get their buy-in is to get them involved in the process. You can encourage parents to do this by getting the Rainbow Resource or other homeschool catalog and handing it to their teen. Parents can tell them they've already picked out their math and language programs but that they'd like the teen to help choose the science program that looks good to them. The catalog will have a collection of different homeschool curriculum so teens can see the variety and a brief description of each.

Alternately, parents can narrow it down to two science programs that they like and say, "I've found these two science programs. I'd like you to have more control over your education. Which one do you like best?"

Parents can also get creative. One year, I gave my oldest a copy of the table of contents from a biology textbook and said to use her artistic skills to make her own textbook that covered these topics. Using a composition notebook, she created her own version of a textbook with research done at the library and her own drawings. This was perfect for her learning style.

A lot of times I talk to parents about teaching high

school and they say, "Well, I know my child isn't going to college." While they may know this about their child, if possible, encourage them to set up for success at college anyway. They can do this by looking at the graduation requirements for your state. If your state only requires 3 years of math to graduate, but your local college requires 4 years of math, it's better to do the 4 years. This way they can enter college with no problems. Without this, they may have to take remedial classes or have trouble being admitted into certain universities.

Children will rise to the level of your expectations.

Not every child can handle the course load of a typical high school student.

Each child has a specific set of needs and if a teen has a learning disability, then simply graduating with the skills he needs will be a success. However, make sure that parents aren't shortchanging their teen just because it's easier than fighting them to get an excellent education. If parents know why a good education is necessary, then putting in the extra effort will be easier.

Parents can also involve their high school or junior high children by sitting down with them and asking some questions.

- What things do you want to do this year? (Get a job? Learn to drive? Go to camp? Learn to code?)

- What do you want to do when you graduate? (Go to college? Go to work? Graduate early?)
- What are you interested in? (Video games? Photography? Fashion? News reporting?)
- How can we help you make those things happen? (Go get your permit from the DMV? Get a part-time job to earn money for camp? Find a good English program so you can become a reporter?)

After several months of high school, encourage parents to visit their local community college's website to find out about entry requirements and dual enrollment options.

Vicki Says:

ONCE YOUR KIDS are middle school-ish or above, their *I don't want to* can be not only *I can't,* but also *I'm bored* or *I'm miserable* or *I'm never going to use this, so why bother?*

Let's be honest. Do you really want to do something for hours a day, every day, just because someone else tells you what to do, how to do it, and when to do it? You probably want to have some choice in what and when and how. And you want it to be relevant to your life, one way or another. If not, it's simply busywork.

Maybe your teen doesn't want to learn math, but he *does* want to start a lawn care business or paint his room or design a video game or be able to figure out if his future paycheck is correct or his investments are wise. If he can see that he will need those math skills—even if he isn't thrilled about learning them—you have salted his proverbial "oats" and now he's thirsty! Learning is now relevant.

For our teens, motivation, perseverance, and diligence are often linked to relevance and choices.[12] If removing that math course from the equation doesn't add up for your student's plan right now (see what I did there?), can you give him a choice in which course he takes? Can you let him choose between online or text or in-person class? Can he decide whether he does it first thing in the morning or late at night? Choices empower our students to take ownership of their learning. You can minimize the power struggle by giving your student as much autonomy as he shows he can handle.

Chapter 10

What Else do I Need to Know?

John Taylor Gatto made a list of things he felt education should produce. While his list is meant to be read to a senate committee, this shortened version will give you an idea of what he thought education should look like.

I'll paraphrase:

- Educated people don't have trouble finding something to do and don't mind being alone.
- Educated people understand people so they have good relationships and interactions.
- Educated people understand their life is temporary and try to learn from those around them.
- Educated people are aware of the values and

cultures of the world and have formed their own set of values to live by.
- Educated people love to create new things and discover truth through exploration and evidence.
- Educated people notice other people's needs and find a way to meet those needs in a way that produces well-paid work and employment. They also realize that love, curiosity, honor and empathy don't cost money and produce happiness.
- Educated people seek variety. They find pleasure and knowledge in different things, but understand that without a home and responsibilities, variety is empty.
- Educated people ask themselves the deep questions like; Who am I? Where are my limits? What am I capable of? Which version of myself do I show in each situation?
- Educated people examine the physical world, study, investigate, and test it.
- Educated people wrestle with family relationships, friendships, companionships, comradeship, love, hate, community, and networking.
- Educated people contemplate the best way to contribute to the common good while simultaneously earning a living doing so.

- Educated people study death, the final act of life, realizing they are mortal and that leaving a legacy to the next generation is powerful.

Afterword: Can You Just Tell Parents What to do?

If you'd like to give parents some in-depth help designing their homeschool plan or if they've been homeschooling for a while and would like some additional guidance, let them know about my book, *Help! I Just Pulled My Kids Out of School: Guidance from 17 Years of Homeschooling* and that they can also use the form at NinaHelpsYou-Homeschool.com to book a one-on-one consultation with me.

About the Author

After 17 years of homeschooling their children, Nina and her husband have two happy adult kids and one not yet graduated. All three children have different personalities and strengths.

Nina has also homeschooled special needs foster children, created homeschool support groups, been a homeschool speaker, mentored new homeschool moms, owned a home business and is a bestselling author under another name.

Acknowledgments

Thank you Vicki, Jessica and Laura for contributing your voices. I'm grateful to the entire team at Zamiz Press for making this book a success.

Recommended Reading

Recommended Reading for Homeschool Parents

- *Weapons of Mass Instruction* by John Taylor Gatto
- *The Vanishing American Adult* by Ben Sasse
- *The Read-Aloud Handbook* by Jim Trelease
- *The Power of Habit* by Charles Duhigg
- *Atomic Habits* by James Clear
- *Outliers* by Malcolm Gladwell
- *The Underground History of American Education: Volume One* by John Taylor Gatto
- *Blackout* by Candace Owens
- *The Lost Tools of Learning* by Dorothy Sayers

Additional Reading

- *Battle for the American Mind* by Pete Hegseth
- *Atlas Shrugged* by Ayn Rand
- *Over the Top* by Zig Ziglar
- *Failing Forward* by John Maxwell
- *The Tipping Point* by Malcolm Gladwell

Tools, Support, and Advice for New Homeschooling Parents

Endnotes

Endnotes

1. Baltimore: https://www.theblaze.com/news/zero-students-proficient-in-math-in-23-baltimore-schools-test-results-reveal?fbclid=IwAR2_uUlpc3ByTBKO7TePqC58n-VFCvLMjMSJt-aKYSxIKjJp2dAQPvuiaWk#toggle-gdpr
2. Ukraine: https://republicanwatch.com/ukrainian-refugee-wants-to-leave-after-two-months-in-san-francisco/?fbclid=IwAR3XPkmgFmO6IZahQnWOzk6d1Bz86XcTJenGiGcporbu2Cshn9J_QoyVizQ
3. San Francisco: https://www.sfexaminer.com/news/education/another-sf-middle-school-falls-

into-disciplinary-chaos/article_468ccbce-9095-11ed-a69c-1b42852679ae.html
4. Dr. Susan Berry: https://www.aop.com/blog/why-colleges-are-recruiting-homeschoolers
5. Peterson, Jordan. *12 Rules for Life*. Random House Canada, 2018.
6. Ziglar, Zig. *Over the Top*. 2nd ed., Thomas Nelson, 1997.
7. Fast growing: https://projects.propublica.org/graphics/homeschool
8. Legality: https://hslda.org/post/answers-to-your-most-pressing-homeschooling-questions
9. Gatto, John Taylor. *Weapons of Mass Instruction*. New Society Publishers, 2009.
10. Department of Education: https://nces.ed.gov/pubs2017/2017102.pdf
11. *Battle for the American Mind,* Pete Hegseth, Harper Collins 2022 [Quote emphasis mine]
12. "Character." Merriam-Webster.com Dictionary, Merriam-Webster, https://www.merriam-webster.com/dictionary/character. Accessed 20 Apr. 2023.
13. Charlotte Mason: https://simplycharlottemason.com
14. Susan Wise Bauer: https://welltrainedmind.com/a/classical-education/
15. Classical education: https://classicalacademicpress.com/pages/what-is-classical-education

Endnotes

16. Social interaction: https://www.nheri.org/a-systematic-review-of-the-empirical-research-on-selected-aspects-of-homeschooling-as-a-school-choice/
17. Sonlight: https://www.sonlight.com/homeschool/curriculum

Elliot Tanner: https://www.theepochtimes.com/after-2-years-homeschooling-using-high-school-curriculum-boy-13-graduates-college-with-3-78-gpa_446991.html?ea_src=open&ea_med=search

Kip & Mona Lisa Harding: https://www.theepochtimes.com/brainy-bunch-parents-homeschool-their-10-kids-with-all-of-them-graduating-high-school-at-12_4210059.html?ea_src=ai&ea_med=search

Lost Tools of Learning: https://logosschool.com/wp-content/uploads/2011/09/LOST-TOOLS-CHART.pdf

"Vicki Says" Endnotes

1. Robin Sampson, *The Heart of Wisdom*

Endnotes

Teaching Approach, Heart of Wisdom Publishing, 2005

2. Bentley, "Life is Messy," https://everydayhomemaking.com/life-is-still-messy/
3. Bentley, "Jump-start to Joyful Motherhood," Alliance Recordings, https://www.alliancerecordings.com/detail.cfm?context=Recordings&SpeakerID=27&RID=2174
4. Bentley, "Is My Child Ready to Read?" https://everydayhomemaking.com/is-my-child-ready-to-read
5. Ginny Yurich, "Play is the Main Occupation of Children," 1000 Hours Outside, https://www.1000hoursoutside.com/blog/play-is-the-main-occupation-of-children-interview-with-angela-hanscom
6. Bentley, "What to Do with Your Young Learner," https://everydayhomemaking.com/what-to-do-with-your-young-learner/
7. Rebekah McBride, Strewing article https://nodeskrequired.com/what-is-strewing
8. Rachel Ramey, "Unschooling—What Inspires Learning?" Titus 2 Homemaker, https://titus2homemaker.com/unschooling-what-inspires-learning/
9. Vicki Bentley, "Suddenly Homeschooling: The Basics," Everyday Homemaking, https://everydayhomemaking.com/SuddenlyHomeschooling-TheBasics

Endnotes

10. Rachel Ramey, "I Hated Homeschooling," Everyday Homemaking, https://everydayhomemaking.com/i-hated-homeschooling/
11. Bentley, "Suddenly Homeschooling: The Basics" https://everydayhomemaking.com/SuddenlyHomeschooling-TheBasics
12. Bentley, "Making the Most of the Middle School Years," https://everydayhomemaking.com/making-the-most-of-the-middle-school-years/

Learning Language Arts Through Literature

- Complete integrated program for 1st–12th grades
- Each level covers: reading, vocabulary, grammar, writing, spelling, and more using real literature
- Affordable, effective, easy-to-use!

Try four full lessons from each level for free!

Common Sense Press
Simple to teach. Easy to learn.

commonsensepress.com

Award-Winning PreK-12+ Curriculum!

Affordable and easy to use!

FREE Shipping +20% Off!

Visit: www.criticalthinking.com/special-offers

Free Critical Thinking Puzzle of the Week!

Emailed, No Purchase Necessary
Visit:
www.criticalthinking.com/vicki

The Critical Thinking Co.™
—Empower the mind!

Homeschool
with Confidence

Vicki Bentley

Exploring Homeschooling:
10 Common Questions

So You've Decided to Homeschool...Now What?
1-hr video "crash course"

Homeschool Blog Posts

Personal Consultation Services

> You and I only know to do what WE did....so we re-create school at home. But homeschooling is so much more than just school-at-home....
>
> *It's a lifestyle of learning*
>
> — VICKI BENTLEY

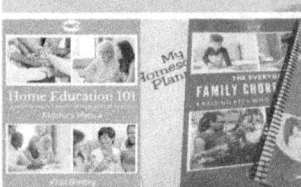

Home Ed 101 books
Mentoring manuals for groups
Parent workbooks for Home Ed 101
Homeschool with Confidence
My Homeschool Planner
Everyday Family Chore System

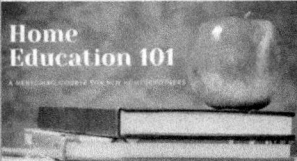

Home Education 101
6-week online course

Other Online Courses
courses.homeschoolwithconfidence.com

Everyday homeschooling
Follow us on Facebook

www.homeschoolwithconfidence.com
www.everydayhomemaking.com
www.vickibentley.com

Additional Titles From

ZAMIZ PRESS

Sophia Wants to Write a Book

The book kids write themselves! Put your name on the cover. Add your "about the author" photo. Help Sophia write a book and become a real author today.

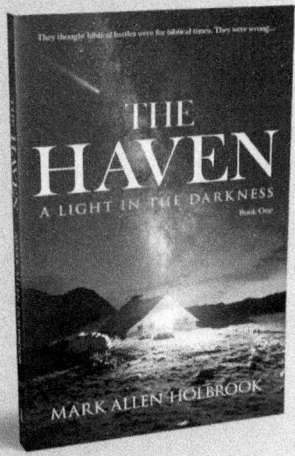

The Haven: A Light in the Darkness

- Twelve friends
- The world falling apart
- A mission from God

ZamizPress.com Publishing With Integrity

www.ingramcontent.com/pod-product-compliance
Lightning Source LLC
Chambersburg PA
CBHW072036110526
44592CB00012B/1446